Nyansa Classical Community Year One Literature Workbook
Copyright © 2025 by Nyansa Classical Community

Published in the United States by Nyansa Classical Community
2416 S. Derbigny St.
New Orleans, LA 70125
nyansaclassicalcommunity.org

To order additional materials, please go to
www.nyansaclassicalcommunity.org

ISBN 978-1-967443-02-4 (paperback)
ISBN: 978-1-967443-03-1 (eBook)

Cover design by Laura Duffy
Book design by Sarah Scudder
Illustrations by Josslyn Littles and Eve Singer
Content developed by Dr. Angel Adams Parham
Greek Myth poetry written by Ahnia Leary

Printed in the United States of America

CREDITS

All literature images created by Josslyn Littles and Eve Singer
Greek Myth poetry written by Ahnia Leary

ACKNOLWEDGEMENTS

Thank you to the following organization for their support and funding:

NYANSA CLASSICAL COMMUNITY

Founded by Dr. Angel Adams Parham, Nyansa Classical Community provides classical, Christian curricula and programming designed to connect with and draw students from diverse backgrounds into the beauty of classical literature and the Great Conversation. For more information, please go to nyansaclassicalcommunity.org.

NYANSA MATERIALS

This workbook is intended to be used alongside our Year One Elementary Curricula. This book should be purchased with Nyansa Teacher's Guide and Year One Elementary Lesson Books.
To order additional materials please go to: www.nyansaclassicalcommunity.org

DEMETER - GREEK GODDESS OF THE EARTH

COPYWORK

Copy the virtue sentence below.

Love is caring for a person or thing very much and wishing good towards them.

COPYWORK

Copy the vice sentence below.

Hate is disliking a person or thing very much and wishing harm towards them.

NARRATION

Write a narration of the Greek Myth story below. Include as many details as you can.

COPYWORK

Copy the memory sentence below.

Demeter loved Persephone and got her back from Hades.

Draw a picture to illustrate today's memory sentence.

BRAINSTORMING

Copy words and ideas from today's brainstorming activity.

DICTATION

MEMORIZE

Memorize the poem below.

THE GODDESS DEMETER

A beautiful goddess of Heaven and rebirth,
Demeter was known to be a mother to the Earth,
Flowers bloomed from her beauty and love,
She was a powerful goddess in the sky above.
Her daughter Persephone loved nature and the sun,
Through the meadows and fields she was delighted to run.
Until one day Hades wanted a wife,
He begged Zeus to give him part of her life.
Persephone was doomed to the underworld,
Demeter had lost her lovely little girl.
She cried and cried for three months straight,
Because Persephone was doomed to a gloomy fate.
From Hades Pomegranate were three berries she ate.
And now winter lasts three full months long,
When Demeter cries, not a smile nor song.
The other nine months are filled with cheer,
Because spring, summer, and Persephone is here!

POEM

Record your poem here.

APHRODITE - GREEK GODDESS OF LOVE

COPYWORK

Copy the virtue sentence below.

Compassion is feeling sorry for those who are suffering and wanting to help.

COPYWORK

Copy the vice sentence below.

Indifference is ignoring the suffering or needs of others.

NARRATION

Write a narration of the Greek Myth story below. Include as many details as you can.

COPYWORK

Copy the memory sentence below.

Compassionate Aphrodite helped Melanion beat swift Atalanta in a race.

Draw a picture to illustrate today's memory sentence.

BRAINSTORMING

Copy words and ideas from today's brainstorming activity.

DICTATION

MEMORIZE

Memorize the poem below.

APHRODITE

Adorned with roses, dressed in pink,
Flowing with beauty after ever blink
As gentle as doves in the skies above,
Aphrodite was the goddess of beauty and love

As gentle as the petals of lovely flowers,
Her mission was always to uplift and empower,
Determined to save Atalanta's fate,
Aphrodite vowed to bring love, not hate.

Atalanta was determined to never get married,
She was the fastest runner, and knew the power she carried,
In the race for her heart, countless princes tried,
But each one lost, and was sentenced to die!

Until one day Prince Melonian approached,
Aphrodite decided to become his coach.
She gave him gold to win Atalanta's heart,
So the two fell in love, and would never part.

POEM

Record your poem here.

ARES - GREEK GOD OF WAR

COPYWORK

Copy the virtue sentence below.

Forgiveness is not holding someone else's bad actions against them.

COPYWORK

Copy the vice sentence below.

Vengeance is trying to make someone suffer because of their actions towards you.

NARRATION

Write a narration of the Greek Myth story below. Include as many details as you can.

COPYWORK

Copy the memory sentence below.

Ares' daughter Penthesilea tried to take revenge on Achilles but failed.

Draw a picture to illustrate today's memory sentence.

BRAINSTORMING

Copy words and ideas from today's brainstorming activity.

DICTATION

MEMORIZE

Memorize the poem below.

ARES

Greek god of vengeance, courage, and war,
Never remembering what he was truly fighting for,
Too blinded by pride to admit when he was wrong,
Ares loved bloodshed like birds love songs.

The great Trojan War lasted 10 years,
Filled with much pain, turmoil, and tears.
Penthesilea, Ares own flesh and blood,
Was too eager to battle amongst swords and mud.

She boasted that she could defeat each and every Greek,
She sought the most glory that a god could seek.
But she was quickly humbled when it was time for war,
When Achilles came with power she had never seen before

Upon hearing of the terrible tragedy with his daughter,
Ares summoned the rage of a father
He brought more destruction on the city of Troy
Vengeance was the only source of his joy.

POEM

Record your poem here.

HERA- GREEK QUEEN OF THE GODS

COPYWORK

Copy the virtue sentence below.

Kindness is treating others with respect, gentleness, and compassion.

COPYWORK

Copy the vice sentence below.

Cruelty is hurting others on purpose.

NARRATION

Write a narration of the Greek Myth story below. Include as many details as you can.

COPYWORK

Copy the memory sentence below.

Hera cruelly rejected her own son Hephaestus because he was lame.

Draw a picture to illustrate today's memory sentence.

BRAINSTORMING

Copy words and ideas from today's brainstorming activity.

DICTATION

MEMORIZE

Memorize the poem below.

THE GODDESS HERA

Hera, the lovely, godly queen,
Was driven by anger and often mean.
After her father nearly took her life,
She was FORCED to become Zeus's wife.
Goddess of women, marriage, and the stars,
Her marriage felt like she was stuck behind bars.
With Zeus always longing for other women,
Anger and betrayal fueled her decisions.
When she found out Zeus had another love,
Unrest lingered in the skies above.
She even found out he had a child on his own,
Which made her feel even more caged and alone.
Hera gave birth to Hephaestus in spite,
But she banned and shamed him with all her might.
He grew up to be the mighty god of fire,
And got revenge on his mother and her bitter desire.

POEM

Record your poem here.

APOLLO - GREEK GOD OF MUSIC AND ARCHERY

COPYWORK

Copy the virtue sentence below.

Humility is acknowledging your own flaws and recognizing the gifts of others.

COPYWORK

Copy the vice sentence below.

Arrogance is thinking you are much better than other people.

NARRATION

Write a narration of the Greek Myth story below. Include as many details as you can.

COPYWORK

Copy the memory sentence below.

Eros punished arrogant Apollo by making him fall in love.

Draw a picture to illustrate today's memory sentence.

BRAINSTORMING

Copy words and ideas from today's brainstorming activity.

DICTATION

MEMORIZE

Memorize the poem below.

APOLLO

Many say that the god Apollo,
Had a heart that wasn't full, but hollow.
Skilled god of music and archery,
Apollo could also predict the future, telling the prophecies.

Blessed with the accuracy of his bow and arrow,
His weapons hit their targets with the grace of a sparrow
He mocked young Eros for claiming his skills could compare,
But Eros simply plotted, with a plan and a glare.

One day he shot Apollo with the arrow of love,
Forcing him to fall in love with Daphne, a river nymph above.
But Daphne was shot with the arrow of hate,
That would lead to the demise of Apollo's fate.

No matter how many times he tried and tried,
Each time Apollo courted Daphne, she would run away and hide!
She begged her father to turn her into a laurel tree,
Lonely and heartbroken would Apollo always be.

POEM

Record your poem here.

ATHENA - THE GODDESS OF WEAVING

COPYWORK

Copy the virtue sentence below.

Wisdom is knowing the right thing to do in every different situation.

COPYWORK

Copy the vice sentence below.

Foolishness is making bad decisions and ignoring good advice.

NARRATION

Write a narration of the Greek Myth story below. Include as many details as you can.

COPYWORK

Copy the memory sentence below.

Arachne foolishly mocked Athena.

Draw a picture to illustrate today's memory sentence.

BRAINSTORMING

Copy words and ideas from today's brainstorming activity.

DICTATION

MEMORIZE

Memorize the poem below.

THE GODDESS ATHENA

Treasured goddess of wisdom and war,
Blessed with the skills worth fighting for,
Born straight out of Zeus's head,
Athena was always one step ahead.

One day she picked up her cloth to weave.
When she heard things she could not believe!
A girl named Arachne was challenging her skill,
Ignoring that her talents came from the goddess's will.

So Athena came down in a tricky disguise,
Determined to hear Arachne's lies.
She revealed herself, and challenged her to a test,
To see who could really weave the best.

Arachne couldn't manage to hide her disrespect,
Her weaving was filled with insult and neglect.
Athena wouldn't be insulted beside her,
So she punished Arachne, turning her to a spider!

POEM

Record your poem here.

ZEUS - GREEK GOD OF HEAVEN

COPYWORK

Copy the virtue sentence below.

Justice is giving to each person what they deserve.

COPYWORK

Copy the vice sentence below.

Injustice is keeping from others what rightfully belongs to them.

NARRATION

Write a narration of the Greek Myth story below. Include as many details as you can.

COPYWORK

Copy the memory sentence below.

Zeus justly punished Tantalus for his crimes.

Draw a picture to illustrate today's memory sentence.

BRAINSTORMING

Copy words and ideas from today's brainstorming activity.

DICTATION

MEMORIZE

Memorize the poem below.

KING ZEUS

There once was a king of many gods,
With strength and power from a lightning rod.
His knowledge of law and justice put to use,
The god of Mount Olympus was named King Zeus!

There also was a king named Tantalus who lived in the lands of Earth,
He was an evil man, guided by greed and wealth since birth.
One day after eating with the gods in heaven,
Tantalus was filled with a mind for aggression.

He would host a dinner for everyone,
And planned to serve plates of his very own son!
The gods were unaware of his trickery and spite,
Demeter even accidentally took a bite!

Zeus was outraged, as were the gods and his wife,
He quickly brought the poor boy back to life.
Determined to punish Tantalus for his horrendous crime,
Zeus sentenced him to be hungry and thirsty until the end of time.

POEM

Record your poem here.

ARTEMIS - GREEK GODDESS OF HUNTING

COPYWORK

Copy the virtue sentence below.

Gratitude is being thankful for all things and blessing others.

COPYWORK

Copy the vice sentence below.

Jealousy is hating others and wanting what they have for yourself.

NARRATION

Write a narration of the Greek Myth story below. Include as many details as you can.

COPYWORK

Copy the memory sentence below.

Artemis accidentally shot her beloved Orion.

Draw a picture to illustrate today's memory sentence.

BRAINSTORMING

Copy words and ideas from today's brainstorming activity.

DICTATION

MEMORIZE

Memorize the poem below.

ARTEMIS

As swift and graceful as a sparrow,
Especially skilled with a bow and arrow,
Beautiful, fierce, and fearful of nothing,
Artemis is known as the goddess of hunting.

One day while hunting in the forest for all,
She met a handsome man nearly 70 feet tall!
Walking on water, skilled with a bow
Orion showed Artemis all the love he could show.

Together they hunted and sped through the woods
Tracking down all the animals they could
Apollo was jealous and quickly got mad
He wanted what Orion and his sister had.

He took Artemis for target practice by the sea,
But didn't tell her what the target would be
No sorrow could match the pain she felt
When Orion left the world to be Orion's Belt.

POEM

Record your poem here.

PROMETHEUS - A TITAN

COPYWORK

Copy the virtue sentence below.

Self-discipline is being able to do the right thing even when tempted to do something else.

COPYWORK

Copy the vice sentence below.

Indiscipline is acting without considering the consequences.

NARRATION

Write a narration of the Greek Myth story below. Include as many details as you can.

COPYWORK

Copy the memory sentence below.

Prometheus was punished by Zeus for giving fire to mankind.

Draw a picture to illustrate today's memory sentence.

BRAINSTORMING

Copy words and ideas from today's brainstorming activity.

DICTATION

MEMORIZE

Memorize the poem below.

PROMETHEUS

Technically a Titan, different from a god,
Unarmed with a lightning bolt, trident, or rod,
Assigned to create all the creatures on Earth,
Prometheus controlled every humans' birth.

He gave the gift of fire to all of mankind,
Though they acted like they had lost their minds!
Zeus was furious, and punished the titan
While his brother watched from a distance, frightened.

Zeus wanted to punish Epimetheus too
He had a cunning plan, and knew just what to do.
He crafted a woman named Pandora for his wife,
And filled her with the gifts to destroy human life.

One day her curiosity was too much to contain
She opened the gift box, and released a world of pain
The gods gifts flew back to heaven, except for one to cope
The humans on earth were left with hope.

POEM

Record your poem here.

PROMETHEUS - A TITAN

COPYWORK

Copy the virtue sentence below.

Heroism is using your strength or knowledge to help and protect others.

COPYWORK

Copy the vice sentence below.

Exploitation is when you use someone's weakness to hurt them.

NARRATION

Write a narration of the Greek Myth story below. Include as many details as you can.

COPYWORK

Copy the memory sentence below.

Dionysus turned the evil exploiting pirates into dolphins.

Draw a picture to illustrate today's memory sentence.

BRAINSTORMING

Copy words and ideas from today's brainstorming activity.

DICTATION

MEMORIZE

Memorize the poem below.

THE STORY OF DIONYSUS

Many years ago in a far off land
There lived a crazy god of wine, parties, and plants.
Taming animals from tigers to bulls,
Dionysus's cup was always full.

One day on his travels through the sea,
He spotted a monster, could it really be?
The monster turned out to be a pirate ship,
He hoped it would aid him on his long trip.

At first everything seemed fine
Until the sailors changed course, and things started to decline.
Just as Dionysus began to nap,
He realized that he was being kidnapped!

The clever god had many tricks up his sleeve,
He turned the oars into snakes so that he could leave.
Turning all his captors into dolphins but one,
Dionysus was free, and feared no one!

POEM

Record your poem here.

HADES - GOD OF DEATH

COPYWORK

Copy the virtue sentence below.

Generosity is giving whatever you have to others cheerfully.

COPYWORK

Copy the vice sentence below.

Miserliness is selfishly keeping everything you have for yourself.

NARRATION

Write a narration of the Greek Myth story below. Include as many details as you can.

COPYWORK

Copy the memory sentence below.

Asklepios angered Hades by generously healing the sick and injured.

Draw a picture to illustrate today's memory sentence.

BRAINSTORMING

Copy words and ideas from today's brainstorming activity.

DICTATION

MEMORIZE

Memorize the poem below.

HADES OF THE UNDERWORLD

The meanest, grumpiest god of the Greeks,
Known to be a tyrant, preying on the weak,
Snatching souls of those who took their last breath,
Hades was known as the god of death.

He ruled in the depths of the underworld,
His wife Persephone was no more than a girl.
A surprising fact that many don't know,
Was that Hades made jewels and helped crops grow.

One day he got word of the son of a god,
Who was healing the sick, and changing lives abroad.
He cheated death with a medicinal dose,
Hades was determined to stop Asklepios.

He charged him with bringing the dead back to life,
And presented the notion to Zeus and his wife.
Zeus was furious, and had him killed in thin air,
All for starting the practice of healthcare.

POEM

Record your poem here.

HESTIA - GREEK GODDESS OF THE HEARTH

COPYWORK

Copy the virtue sentence below.

Hospitality is welcoming others into your home and looking to serve them.

COPYWORK

Copy the vice sentence below.

Inhospitality is being unwelcoming and rude to others in your home.

NARRATION

Write a narration of the Greek Myth story below. Include as many details as you can.

COPYWORK

Copy the memory sentence below.

Hestia showed hospitality to the gods by protecting the hearth.

Draw a picture to illustrate today's memory sentence.

BRAINSTORMING

Copy words and ideas from today's brainstorming activity.

DICTATION

MEMORIZE

Memorize the poem below.

HESTIA

As loving and nurturing as mother Earth
Goddess Hestia was the goddess of the hearth.
Guardian of fire, tending to family, food, and love
Hestia spread warmth to the world from heaven above.

Always radiating beauty and peace,
Hestia became the darling of all of Greece
Selfless enough to maintain every fire
The hearts of the gods became filled with desire.

Poseidon and Apollo, the most powerful in the land,
Both longed for Hestia, and asked for her hand
She knew that choosing only one would be the start of a war
And couldn't bear to be the reason that the world's heart tore.

She begged Zeus to let her stay single forever
So she could go on blessing the Earth and all its endeavors
She lead a life of service for the rest of her days,
And always made sure to keep the fires ablaze.

POEM

Record your poem here.

HERMES - GREEK GOD OF MESSAGES

COPYWORK

Copy the virtue sentence below.

Industriousness is working hard and well at whatever you have to do.

COPYWORK

Copy the vice sentence below.

Laziness is doing work slowly and badly or refusing to work at all.

NARRATION

Write a narration of the Greek Myth story below. Include as many details as you can.

COPYWORK

Copy the memory sentence below.

Hermes turned lazy Chelone into a tortoise.

Draw a picture to illustrate today's memory sentence.

BRAINSTORMING

Copy words and ideas from today's brainstorming activity.

DICTATION

MEMORIZE

Memorize the poem below.

HERMES

Messenger of the gods and son of the king,
Hermes controlled the travel of everyone and everything
Clever and hardworking to say the least
Hermes was a messenger for every man, woman, and beast.

On the day Zeus and Hera were set to be married
Wedding invitations were all that Zeus carried
He delivered one to to mountain nymph Chelone
Who was extra lazy and always alone.

She threw away the invitation, careless as ever,
Letting it fly through the wind as light as a feather
On the day of the wedding, filled with celebration and gleam
Chelone the nymph was nowhere to be seen.

Hermes sped to her home to use his words to confront her
But resulted in methods a little bit rougher
He threw her in the water, and turned her to shellfish!
She'd carry her home on her back forever, no matter how hard she
wished.

POEM

Record your poem here.

EROS - GREEK GOD OF LOVE

COPYWORK

Copy the virtue sentence below.

Contentment is being happy with what you have.

COPYWORK

Copy the vice sentence below.

Envy is wanting what others have so much that you wish them harm.

NARRATION

Write a narration of the Greek Myth story below. Include as many details as you can.

COPYWORK

Copy the memory sentence below.

Aphrodite's envy led to Eros marrying the woman Psyche.

Draw a picture to illustrate today's memory sentence.

BRAINSTORMING

Copy words and ideas from today's brainstorming activity.

DICTATION

MEMORIZE

Memorize the poem below.

EROS

Known for causing the gods to fall in love,
Curly haired and handsome, with wings to fly above,
Rumored to cause trouble in his mischievous stance,
Eros was the god of marriage and romance.

One day his mother Aphrodite was angry and distraught
At a human girl named Pysche whom she could have fought
Jealous of her beauty, she sent Eros to shoot,
But he had fallen into love that he could not refute.

He visited Psyche in secret, sneaking through the dark
And warned her not to leave a trace, sound, or mark
Soon her sisters came to see her, and instantly boiled with hate
Jealous that a handsome godly husband would not be their fate.

They convinced her to try to kill him, and she nearly did as told
Until she saw his true form, such glory to behold
She worked long and hard to win him back, and overcome such disaster
Until they married in such godly glamor, living happily ever after.

POEM

Record your poem here.

POSEIDON- GREEK GOD OF THE SEA

COPYWORK

Copy the virtue sentence below.

Trustworthiness is being honest and keeping your word.

COPYWORK

Copy the vice sentence below.

Untrustworthiness is telling lies, acting sneakily, or breaking promises.

NARRATION

Write a narration of the Greek Myth story below. Include as many details as you can.

COPYWORK

Copy the memory sentence below.

Poseidon punished Laomedon for breaking his promise.

Draw a picture to illustrate today's memory sentence.

BRAINSTORMING

Copy words and ideas from today's brainstorming activity.

DICTATION

MEMORIZE

Memorize the poem below.

POSEIDON

Keeper of the ocean, king of the sea,
A god much stronger than you and me,
Lead by a chariot, armed with a trident,
The guardian of the water was named Poseidon.

One day with Zeus, Poseidon revolted
But with the strength of lightning, Zeus bolted
As punishment for his disrespect,
He was sentenced to work, surrounded by neglect.

King Laomedon ordered him to build the walls of Troy,
Little did he know, it was only a ploy.
The king refused to pay him back
So Poseidon decided to lead a ruthless attack!

He sent a sea monster to the human world,
And demanded they sacrifice every young girl.
Hercules saved the city, the king was resentful
He lost everything he loved, Poseidon's revenge was successful.

POEM

Record your poem here.

HELIOS - GREEK GOD OF THE SUN

COPYWORK

Copy the virtue sentence below.

Gentleness is being tender and kind with your actions and words.

COPYWORK

Copy the vice sentence below.

Harshness is treating others with cruelty or severity.

NARRATION

Write a narration of the Greek Myth story below. Include as many details as you can.

COPYWORK

Copy the memory sentence below.

Gentle Helios won the contest with Boreas.

Draw a picture to illustrate today's memory sentence.

BRAINSTORMING

Copy words and ideas from today's brainstorming activity.

DICTATION

MEMORIZE

Memorize the poem below.

HELIOS

Great Titan God of the sun,
A product of heaven and earth, second to no one.
He made sure human beings kept their oaths,
Combining the world and the sky, shining light on both.

The sky god Boreas controlled icy winds and snow,
Arrogant in the strength of the wind he would blow,
He challenged Helios in a competition of power,
But his intentions were nothing but pure, and very sour.

They spotted a man on Earth, free of stress,
And attempted to see who could make him undress.
Boreas blew icy cold wind at the man,
Nearly freezing him to death, so he could barely stand.

Helios instead shined warm rays of sun,
Calming the man so he no longer had to run,
He peacefully took a swim in the lake,
Showing that gentleness beats harshness for kindness sake!

POEM

Record your poem here.

HEPHAESTUS- GOD OF METALWORKING

COPYWORK

Copy the virtue sentence below.

Honesty is telling the truth.

COPYWORK

Copy the vice sentence below.

Dishonesty is hiding the truth.

NARRATION

Write a narration of the Greek Myth story below. Include as many details as you can.

COPYWORK

Copy the memory sentence below.

Hephaestus was the Greek god of metalworking and the forge.

Draw a picture to illustrate today's memory sentence.

BRAINSTORMING

Copy words and ideas from today's brainstorming activity.

DICTATION

MEMORIZE

Memorize the poem below.

HEPHAESTUS

Beautifully crafting metal, silver, and gold,
Outcasted by his mother at less than 2 years old
Giving gifts to mortal men, named after fire,
Hephaestus created beautiful things that everyone desired.

Hera didn't believe that he could succeed
She treated him like garbage, such an evil deed.
Thetis and Eurynome were water goddesses from Earth
They cared for Hephaestus like mothers since birth.

Hephaestus grew up with anger in his heart,
He was robbed of his mother, and from Olympus torn apart.
He trapped Hera in a chair, leaving her helpless,
Forcing her to work with him and become selfless.

He went on to dress the best soldiers in battle,
Hand-crafting lovely chariots, weapons, and saddles.
Adorning his family in the shiniest gold,
The brilliance of Hephaestus would never grow old.

POEM

Record your poem here.

HERCULES - GREEK HERO

COPYWORK

Copy the virtue sentence below.

Fortitude is staying strong under pressure.

COPYWORK

Copy the vice sentence below.

Faint-heartedness is giving up easily.

NARRATION

Write a narration of the Greek Myth story below. Include as many details as you can.

COPYWORK

Copy the memory sentence below.

Because of his fortitude, Hercules gained immortality.

Draw a picture to illustrate today's memory sentence.

BRAINSTORMING

Copy words and ideas from today's brainstorming activity.

DICTATION

POEM

Record your poem here.

MEDUSA - GREEK MONSTER

COPYWORK

Copy the virtue sentence below.

Courage is doing the right thing even when it's scary.

COPYWORK

Copy the vice sentence below.

Cowardice is letting fear control your actions.

NARRATION

Write a narration of the Greek Myth story below. Include as many details as you can.

COPYWORK

Copy the memory sentence below.

Brave Perseus killed Medusa.

Draw a picture to illustrate today's memory sentence.

BRAINSTORMING

Copy words and ideas from today's brainstorming activity.

DICTATION

MEMORIZE

Memorize the poem below.

MEDUSA

Statues in place of the lives she takes,
Long hair flowing with venomous snakes,
Glancing at her enemies to turn them to stone,
Medusa the monster had no mercy to be shown.

In order for the local king to be wed,
He had to have Medusa's head.
So he sent Perseus on a quest to defeat her,
His instructions were given in a careless blur.

Luckily Athena had the warrior recipes,
And gave Perseus the tools of war, necessities.
Armed with invisibility, wings, and a sword,
For his bravery he should have gotten an award.

Finally be faced Medusa in a deep dark cave,
And cut off her head with his sword and a wave.
Given to Athena was her head still filled with power,
Perseus lived on with godly favor every hour.

POEM

Record your poem here.

MEDUSA - GREEK MONSTER

COPYWORK

Copy the virtue sentence below.

Joy is enthusiastically enjoying your blessings.

COPYWORK

Copy the vice sentence below.

Despair is giving up hope when things get hard.

NARRATION

Write a narration of the Greek Myth story below. Include as many details as you can.

COPYWORK

Copy the memory sentence below.

Pan brought joy to all the gods.

Draw a picture to illustrate today's memory sentence.

BRAINSTORMING

Copy words and ideas from today's brainstorming activity.

DICTATION

MEMORIZE

Memorize the poem below.

PAN

Greek god of the mountains, controlling joy and fear,
Capable of producing laughter or tears,
Hairy and stout, half goat half man,
The mischievous creature held the name Pan.

His father was Hermes, his mother Penelope of the mountains,
The couple moved peacefully among the slopes and fountains.
When Penelope gave birth, the nurse was filled with fright,
She screamed and ran away with all her might!

The baby born was no normal babe at all,
He had a hairy feet, a beard, and goat legs far too tall!
But Hermes loved him and was filled with joy.
He hurried to the gods to present his new baby boy.

Zeus too fell in love with his unique grandson,
He set him free to live amongst the nymphs and run.
Pan soon fell in love with Echo, winning her heart.
In the mountains they lived, and were never apart.

POEM

Record your poem here.